Double Moon

Constructions & Conversations

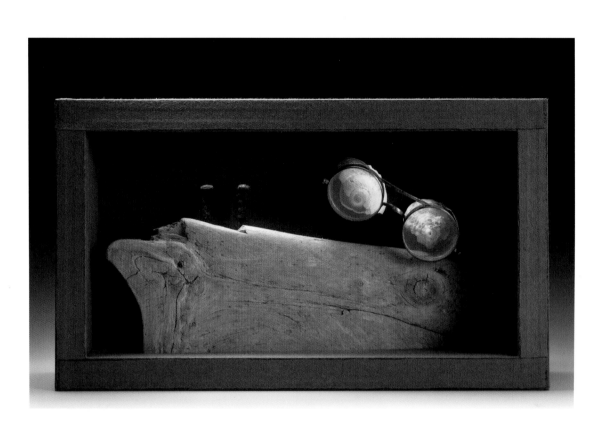

Double Moon

Constructions & Conversations

Constructions by
Margo Klass

Miniature Essays by
Frank Soos

Afterword by
Kesler Woodward

Double Moon: Constructions & Conversations

Constructions copyright © 2009 by Margo Klass
Texts copyright © 2009 by Frank Soos
Afterword copyright © 2009 Kesler Woodward

Photos of art by Chris Arend with these exceptions:
Pages 3, 12, and 67: Photos by Blaine Pennington
Pages 29 and 52: Photos by James Barker
Photo of authors by Barry McWayne

Book and cover design by Wanda Chin

ISBN: 9781597091411
Library of Congress Catalogue Card Number: 200893502

Published by Boreal Books
www.borealbooks.org

First Edition
Printed in China

For Grace

In Memoriam

Table of Contents

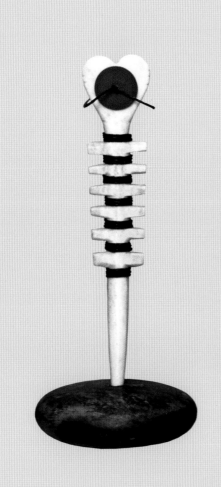

Preface

Do you have trouble quieting your mind?

My psychologist pal Mike asked me that as he began to teach me to meditate away high blood pressure with the help of a thermometer purchased from a car parts store. It never occurred to me that in some unexplored way a quiet mind was a desirable thing to have.

What is the noise the brain makes when it's left turned on? Thrum and clank. The noise coming up the ridgeline from Bluestone, where the N&W coal train ran along the river and through the tunnel into West Virginia. Black on black, the squeal of steel on steel as the wheels of the empty hopper cars leaned into the curving rails. The loose chain banging among the couplers, the monochrome blare of the diesel horn. Heard in the night but not seen from my boyhood bed. Once the train had rumbled through the tunnel, I was left awake in my attic room where the long shadows from the streetlight outside made a shape-shifting invitation to imagine.

Inside the kind of junk store Margo likes to frequent, everything is a jumble. What's the value of a place where everything is ordered and named, is a known quantity with a fixed price? Much better are the places where coffee cans full of old tools, lost keys, bits of brass or steel that used to be good for something but nobody quite remembers what. In that kind of place, Margo will start picking up the pieces in her hand and putting them together in her head. It is there that disparate junk begins to make sense.

Left to its own devices, the mind goes all over the place—past, present, future, the real and the imagined—but wherever it goes, it sets out to make meaning whether there was anything meaningful in the first place or not.

Some shapes might speak to Margo in an archetypal way: The shape of an egg. A beach on one of Maine's ocean-facing islands is filled with egg-shaped rocks. Margo has sorted through hundreds, collecting certain of them for her constructions. And she has used darning eggs, egg-like ceramic test tiles, and real eggs themselves to play on this shape. Put an approximately round object in a squared off box and you get two shapes that want to talk to each other about how they are different, how the space between them grows thick and thin, how such a space is only partly visible to a person looking in.

Other shapes present themselves as well. What they have in common, regardless of their density, their complexity, is that they all want to talk to each other about the space they hold and the space between them.

What's that behind some of those shapes, those places we cannot see but our minds will wander into? Sometimes Margo uses windows and mirrors to invite a person into these spaces. Sometimes, though, there is the tease of space that exists beyond where our senses can take us. In, around, through, and sometimes out the other side.

Then what? Margo wondered if I might want to write responses to her shoebox-sized constructions. Margo's earliest constructions were conscious of their own narrative possibilities. I could respond directly to her intent. Or I could not. As time went on, abstractions set in, wanderings in both word and image went farther afield….

It's the nature of Margo's work to be crisp and precise. Her art is to bring order to the apparent disorder of the discovered world. My aim, it sometimes seems, is to resist order insofar as possible.

In the course of our collaboration, I've returned more than once to the Euclidean problem of squaring the circle. Apparently, it can't be done. And that's what makes it appealing to me. Restless eye syndrome? When I look at the egg in the box, my eye cannot come to rest.

So it happened that a few months after Margo left me with her images, I offered my responses. Pushing and pulling, we considered how image and word worked, how together they more than doubled our intentions, sometimes by accident, sometimes by design. Whatever we were doing, it seemed to be working.

Thrum. Clank. Squeal. Some of the sounds the brain makes when it's left turned on, some of the images sparked by its devising.

Frank Soos

Narratives

Something Not at All Myself

How big does an idea have to be before it is really big? Gravity, say? How big before it is bigger than we are? Until we become nothing but facts balled up inside it? I dragged a chair over and stood on it, tried to reach those kinds of ideas, but people told me to think small, that's where the money is. Advertising jingles. Politics. Not God, but God's by-products. Prayer beads, prayer cloths, figurines for the dashboard and yard. Instead, I sat and waited. Lightning, foxfire, sunrise.

I Have Two

Surprising how little it matters, one a little high,
another a little low, one soft and squishy and
sometimes scarcely here at all—when I'm lying in
bed, it seems to recede into the rest of me—the other
hard as a fist, punching me, reminding me it's here.
I'll tell you the truth, I like sleeping naked. I like
myself bare as birth and alive.

Rube

Find the solution to this puzzle and the red ball will spring free. Then what? You'll have a red ball pulled loose from the tricky ins and outs that kept it running from side to side. You'll have a red ball with nothing left to do but get itself lost under the couch.

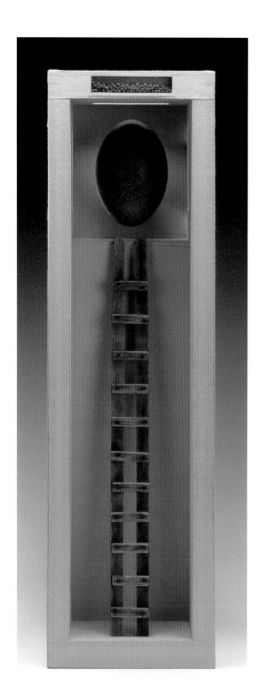

Jacob's Ladder

Why is it that revelation is always granted to the least deserving? Why not to the honest one, the straight-shooter, the maybe not-so-bright one?

But who's to say wisdom should be found in fair play? Could it be the crooked mind finds its way best? If this is so, think what truth must be revealed.

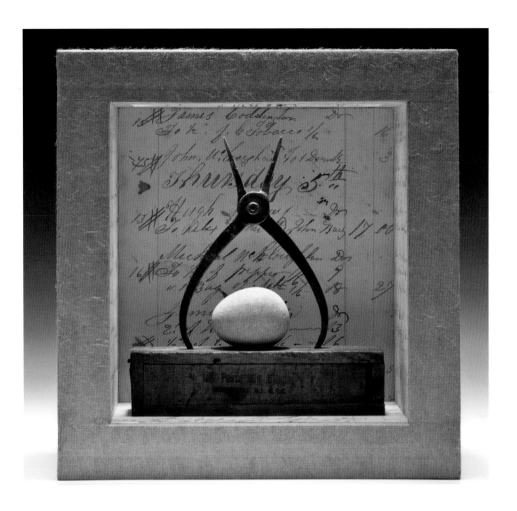

Rock Paper Scissors III

Notice the size of the scissors. We've entered the delicate phase
of the procedure. Yes, there will still be cuts, but they will be
made with greater precision. And the rock? Smaller, too. Made
for a more accurate aim. Will it still hurt? We haven't figured
that part out yet.

Apparently Never

Behind that moustache and silly
grin is just a guy, a guy who buys
only tools with lifetime guarantees,
a guy who will wear a shirt to rags
and then use it for rags. When will
it light up the tiny bulb of his brain:
love is something that might lend
itself to the job at hand, that might
wear itself comfortably in, that might
grow to be a part of who he is?

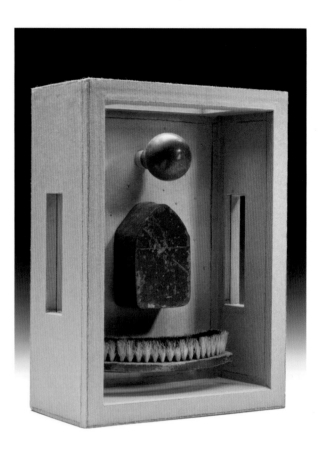

Permanent Press

"I got your nose," my uncle would
say to me, grabbing hold and
twisting, twisting it right off until
there it was sticking out between
two thick fingers. I wanted it back,
of course, not knowing who I'd be
without it.

All I had then was just a nub of a
nose, nothing like the way it would
grow. Given the way it turned out—
too big, too ready to be sniffing into
places where it had no business—
maybe he just should have kept it.

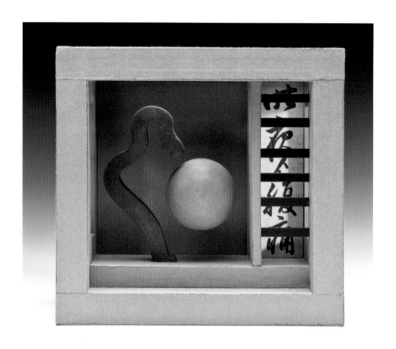

Learning to Love in a Language
We Do Not Understand

We holler to be heard over wind whipping through the
open windows of the truck. "Margot!" I yell to the tape
player's prompting. "Francois!" she yells back across
the windy gulf. "Bonjour!" "Bonsoir!" "Baguette!"
"Croissant!" Unfamiliar shapes fill up my mouth.
"Qu'est-ce que?" Words come out in sounds that aren't
my own. "S'il vous plait. Enchanté." Words come out
that say just what I mean, "Merci. J'taime. Adieu."

Icon

What would the minimum
requirements for sainthood be?
A halo, of course, for effect.
And the shrinkage of the body
to the advantage of the soul.
How little of the one and how
much of the other? At least
a modicum of personhood
remaining? Personhood with all
its attendant needs and wishes,
yes, that would be the problem,
wouldn't it?

Warrior

It's not all it's cracked up to be. I enlisted; the recruiter's
snappy uniform pulled me in. Red is for blood, son, and
gold is for, well, gold. And even the thought it might be
my blood had appeal. I'd sloshed a little out in the bars
and poolrooms a time or two and hadn't missed it much.
Maybe he rolled his pant leg up and showed me the
scar where the rifle ball went right through him on the
battlefield at Austerlitz. Forget it. Men are men, made up
of few fragile parts. The uniforms are replaceable.

Maine

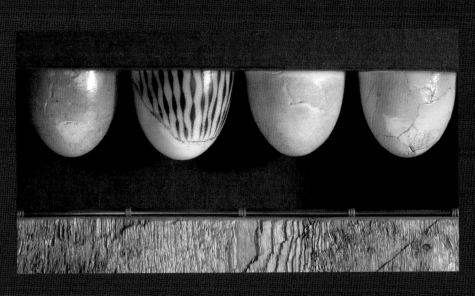

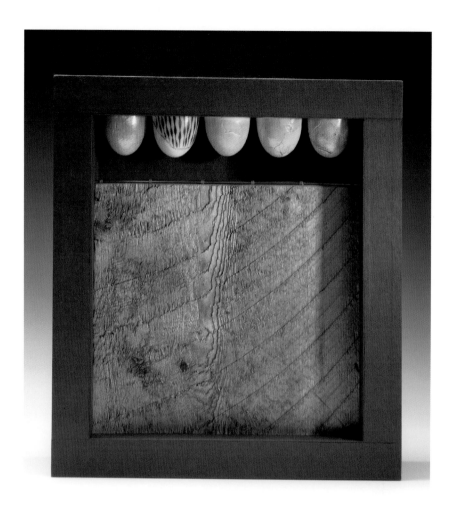

I Dreamed of Ships

I dreamed of ships, decked and timbered, sleek as needles,
angling for home. Spices, tea, wonders brought from elsewhere.
And in their holds, the signatures of the men who made them,
wrought in wood, unwitting agents of surprising gifts, all
answers to my wishes.

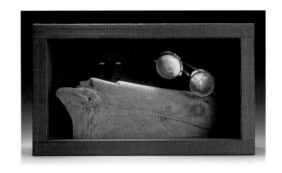

Double Moon

Here is where we all started from, the bottom of the ocean. Down there life was dark and cold and lonesome. What else was there for us, ever hopeful, to do but climb up to the light?

Frail creatures, will we always crave more light? Yes. Right to the dimming end.

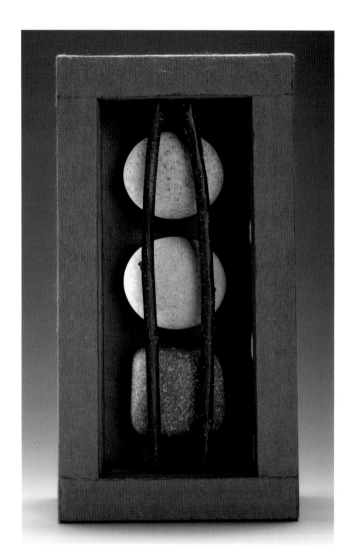

Three

How much of what we come to know as regret is found in the imagination? It's not the past we long for but a future we will never know and will have to guess at. What would these little souls have been bound for? Their prospects seemed as infinite as our wonderings. In this way, their lives can have no limits. In this way we might soothe away our pain.

Breaking Forth

Once people in our town had a pipeline to the Truth.
Then something happened; it broke. Everybody
blamed it on shifting plates down inside the earth.
My dad took me to see, down under the ground,
where fish swam in water-filled caves. They were
in there, he told me as I cast my lure, swimming in
Truth. Blind to anything I had to offer.

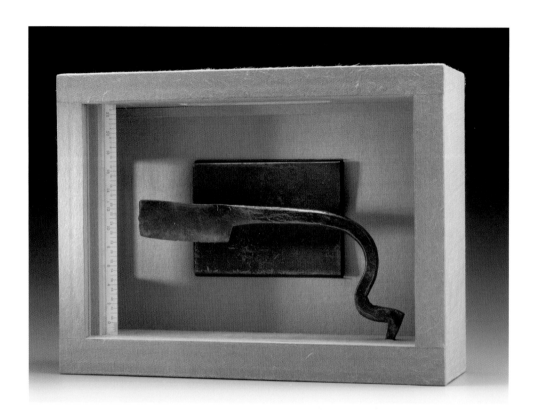

Red Herring

Here's a handy contraption if you happen to
be shopping for a Fate: A measuring device—
you'll notice how abbreviated the increments,
and a not especially sharp guillotine to make
the final cut. And the cloth? The cloth to be cut?
You'll have to supply that yourself.

Staying Still

Where's the glamour in it, all this going here and there? I know what you're thinking: strange buildings and funny-shaped rocks, foods made fresh by spices you've never tasted, creatures you've never seen before except on your TV screen. The way they bury their dead.

What I have come to crave is the morning stillness, the view from this limb onto the meadow below me. The fox and the vole? Confirmation that there's unhappiness to be found everywhere.

I've been there, I've seen it; I know what I know. But what can I do? Travel is bred in my hollow bones when I would just as soon stay here.

Crowley Island Fog

The sea is close at hand
though you might never know.

Though it seems we always
know. The moon above pulls
at the snot-salty blood in our
veins always to remind us
where we came from, having
crawled up onto this rocky
shore, thinking maybe never
to go back.

We can only go back.

Flying Red Point

Faith in the fly is what the fishers call it. Casting, casting,
until casting becomes believing what we offer—a twisting
of feather and fur around a steel hook—will entice what we
think we know to reveal itself. Down on the rocky bottom,
we think they must be there, big ones hiding themselves
until such time as our methodical casting calls them out.

The fly, our hopeful emissary, our homemade notion, our
wrong-headed people's way of always getting on the
wrong end of things.

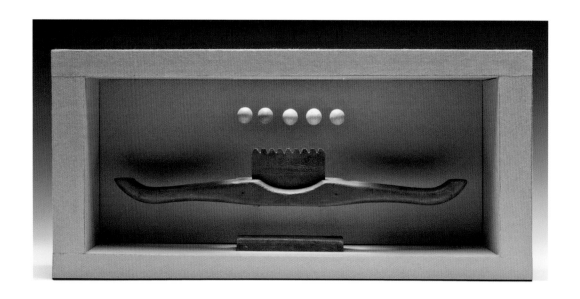

Celestial Navigation

What's so bad about not knowing exactly where you are? To round the corner and be taken by surprise? To look out the window and find a new world is waiting outside? With my driver's license safely in my pocket, I have permission to get out and go, to find a place where I might learn better who I am.

Japan

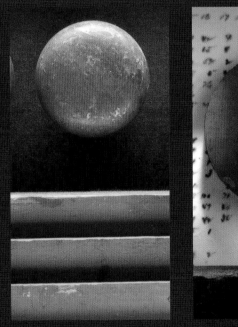
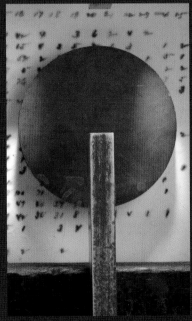

Sugimoto I

Rust has always been the enemy of my life,
always sneaking around, never taking a
break, reminding me that nothing human
ever lasts, reminding me that molecules have
minds of their own.

Rust, I owe you everything.

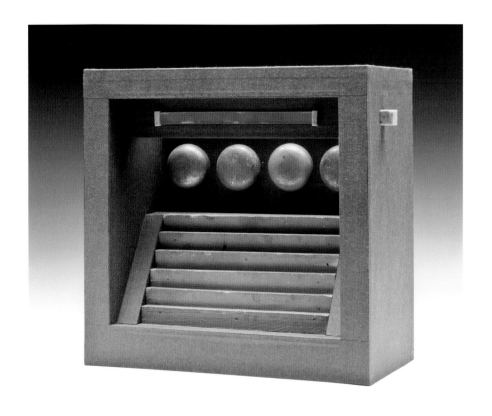

Gate Way

In every science fiction movie there are these
priestly characters worshipfully going around
in expensive bathrobes, climbing the stately
stairs, drawing back the curtain, where the
mystery is revealed: distant, lumpy, and
scarred. A heavenly body as lonely as our own.

Teahouse

I admit I have lived too much of my life there,
running between before and after, wishing and
regretting one and the same. When right now
should be a great pregnant bubble of desire.
Desire big enough to consume my thoughts
away.

Balancing Act

When I was a kid I saw Indian
fakirs on a TV show. They could
stand on one leg for days, weeks,
maybe even years. Me, I couldn't
even walk a rail on the train tracks
for more than a few seconds.
How, I wondered, how to hang on
like that? Then it hit me, the trick,
the willful gift of forgetting I had
two legs.

Window Over the Couch

Sitting on the couch, looking out the window, I see far, landscapes of promise—high, spare mesas, windy deserts, ice caps and glass flat seas. What stands between those places and me? A hole in my pocket, a broken shoelace too short for mending, a warm coat that doesn't fit me.

Tatami Room II

Back on the back wall, a landscape from a distant world lures us in. This would be a tranquil room to spend a quiet hour. Except for that thing, the only possible bit of furniture I see, a thing that would cut us in half, us on one side, our desires on the other.

Site Line

Every now and then, I get a catalog in the mail devoted to opportunities for balance. It offers great big balls for me to sit on, gadgets like pizza pies I can stand on—big ones for both feet, little ones for when I am ready to advance, each foot doing its own individualized balancing act. In this way I will reach deep into my core to find it, find equilibrium and all that must go with it—ease, peace, maybe even joy.

I look at the models sitting on their big balls, rapturous and amazed, gazing into some place I can't see. I want to think it's only a trick of the mind, this balance, a trick I can't get the knack of.

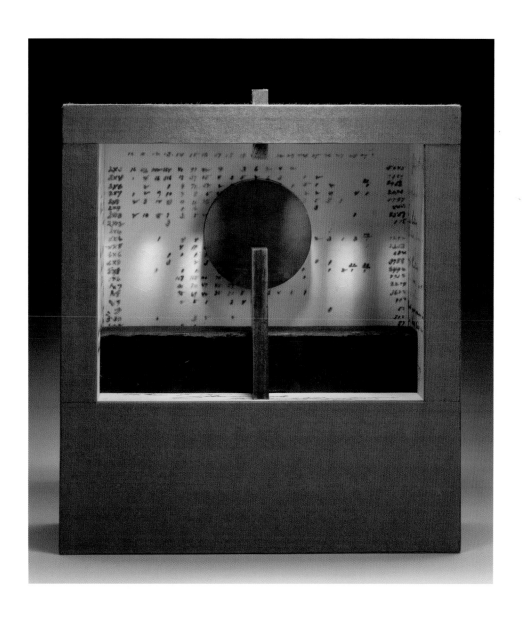

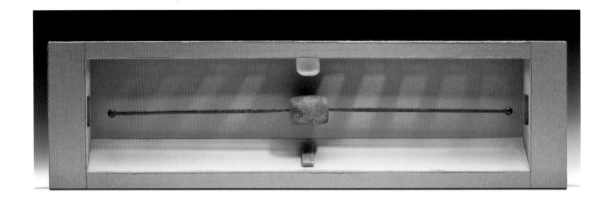

Pavilion

Light really is something. Something that can hit you in
the chest. Hard. That can fall gently to the earth like rain.
Look, it says to us, that sidewalk you travel to the bus
stop every day is not gray at all but is as shot full of color
as a south-facing snowy slope—lavender, pink, and gold.

Altarpieces

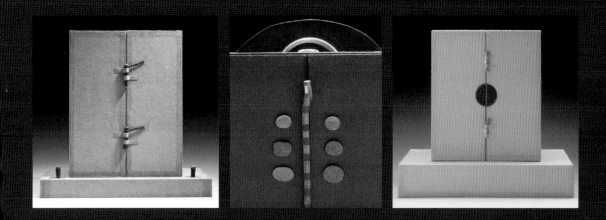

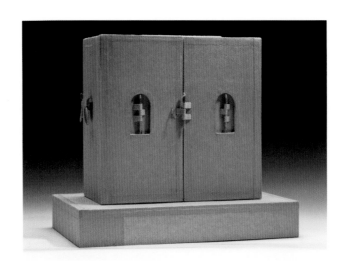

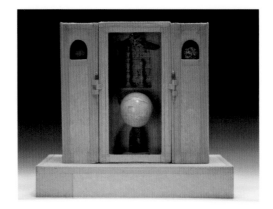

Resurrection

All the gods are present here. How kindly are any of
them disposed to our puny human wishes? With their
attendant saints nearby waiting in adoration, they are a
hard wholeness in themselves. Go ahead, ask for revelation.
They'll grant you what they please.

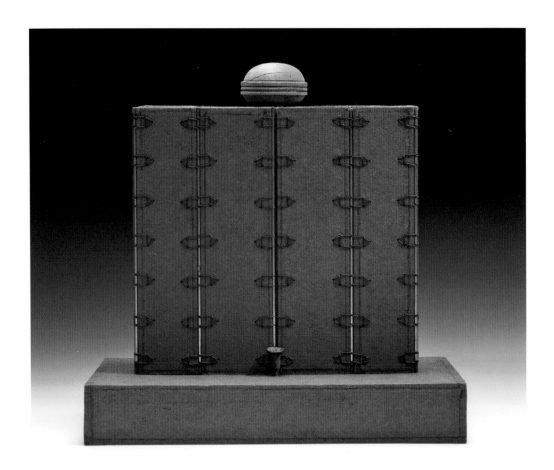

Commerce 123

Steel is not a transcendent material. It will always wind up bowing before gravity; it will always give in to rust. Leave it alone on the ground; it will burrow in and hide itself back where it came from. We build our wishes from steel just the same. We build them into towers and climb.

Look out, birds fly over us.

JANUARY, 1867.

ENDAR FOR N. Y. State, N. Eng-, Wisconsin, Michi-, Iowa and Oregon.

CALEN... New York City;... sylvania, C... diana and Il...

Sun sets.	Moon rises.	High Water Boston	SUN SLOW	MOON'S PLACE	Sun rises	Sun sets	M...
38	3 19	8 26	4		27	7 24 4 44	3
39	4 15	9 15	4		9	7 24 4 45	4
40	5 7	10 0	5		21	7 24 4 46	5
41	5 58	10 50	5		3	7 24 4 47	6
42	sets.	11 36	6		15	7 24 4 48	se

...nday. **Venus in Scorpio.** *Day's*

43	5 47	morn	6		27	7 24 4 49	5
44	6 44	10	7		9	7 24 4 50	6
45	7 42	49	7		21	7 24 4 51	7
46	8 44	1 30	7		3	7 24 4 52	8
47	9 44	2 12	8		17	7 24 4 53	9
48	10 48	2 54	8		30	7 23 4 54	10
49	11 53	3 40	9		14	7 23 4 55	11

...er Epiphany. **Mars in Gemini.** *Day's*

50	morn	4 30	9		27	7 23 4 56	mo
51	58	5 28	9		11	7 22 4 57	2
53	2 5	6 30	10		26	7 22 4 58	2
54	3 13	7 30	10		10	7 22 4 59	3
55	4 19	8 46	10		25	7 21 5 0	4
56	5 24	9 49	11		10	7 21 5 1	5
58	rises.	10 48	11		25	7 20 5 3	ri

...er Epiphany. **Jupiter in Capricorn.** *Day's*

59	5 54	11 40	11		7	19 5 4	5
0	7 0	ev. 28	12		24	7 18 5 5	7
1	8 8	1 14	12		8	7 18 5 6	8
3	9 12	2 1	12		22	7 17 5 8	9
4	10 14	2 45	12		5	7 16 5 9	10
5	11 14	3 28	13		17	7 15 5 10	11
6	morn	4 13	13		30	7 15 5 11	mo

...er Epiphany. **Saturn in Libra.** *Day's*

7	13	5 5	13		12	7 14 5 12	
9	1 10	5 56	13		24	7 13 5 13	1
10	2 6	6 50	13		6	7 12 5 15	2
11	2 59	7 46	14		18	7 12 5 16	2
13	3 52	8 43	14		29	7 11 5 17	3

MOON'S PHASES.

...h. 22 m., evening. | Full Moon, 20th, 2 h. 2...
...11 h. 26 m., morning. | Last Quarter, 27th, 9 h....

...INDIAN VEGETABLE PILLS will c...

MARCH, 1867.

DAR FOR ...State, N. Eng..., ...nnas, Mici..., ...and Oregon.

CA... New J... ...volva... ...ia...

Moon rises.	High Water Boston	SUN SLOW	MOON'S PLACE	Sun rises	s
32	8 7			6 3 5	
4	3 9 0			2 6 3 15	

...dar. **Venus in Sagittarius.**

4 41	9 5	12		14 6 3 25	
5 21	10 36	12		27 6 3 35	
5 57	11 20	12		10 6 3 25	
sets.	11 59	11		23 6 3 75	
7 34	morn	11		7 6 3 25	
8 41	41	11		21 6 3 05	
9 48	1 26	11		5 6 3 22	

...dar. **Mars in Gemini.**

53	2 10	10		19 6 2 95	
0	2 55	10		2 6 2 196	
morn	3 52	10		17 6 2 176	
1	4 54	10		1 6 1 166	
2	6 3	9		16 6 1 146	
2 57	7 16	9		2 6 1 116	
4	8 18	9		16 6 1 116	

...st. **Jupiter in Capricorn.**

4 28	9 17	9		19 6 0 96	
rises.	10 12	8		3 116 7 96	
5 4	10 55	8		18 6 0 66	
6 4	11 37	8		3 6 0 46	
...er.	12	7		2 5 59 3	
8 4	1 0	7		15 5 5 16	
42 14	7		4 5 58 5 6	

...st. **Saturn in Libra.**

10 42	2 41	6		25 5 56 5	
11 32	3 1	6		5 5 56 6	
morn	3 47	5		15 5 54 6	
25	4 38	5		25 5 52 5	
1 12	5 32	5		5 5 51 6	
1 57	6 29	5		27 5 49 6	
2 3	7 26	5		17 5 47 6	

... **Uranus in Gemini.**

| 3 17 | 8 21 | 4 | | 26 5 46 | |

MOON'S PHASES.

...n., morning. | Full Moon, 2d...
...59 m., morning. | Last Quarter,...

...IAN VEGETABLE PILLS...

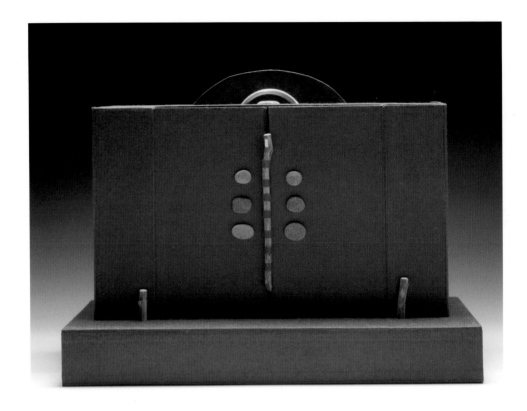

Reliquary of St. Sid: Patron Saint of Surfeit

How might we best save the world? St. Sid thought, perhaps, by taking possession of it stick by stick. By accumulating much more than we could ever use, we might back our way into frugality. To own, to own, to own. The presiding genius of our age, St. Sid taught us the mantra we live by.

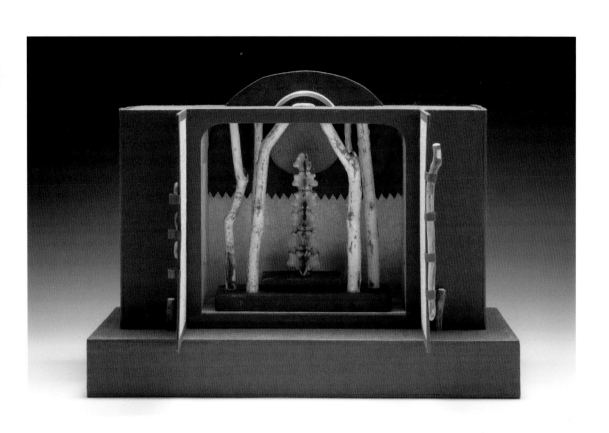

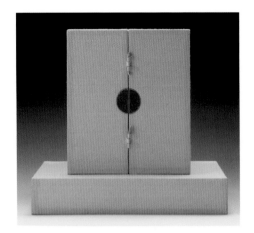

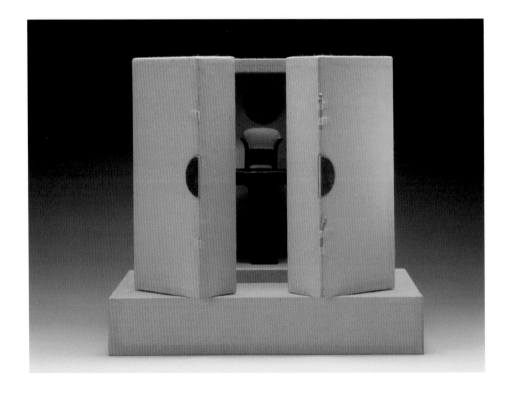

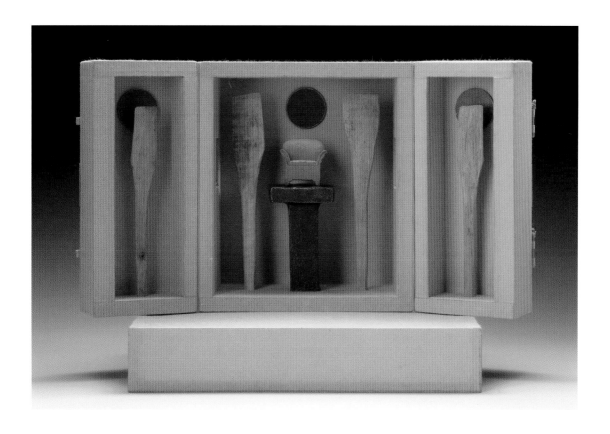

Sanctum Sanctorum

for WCW

Hey, happy genius of your own household, do
kitchen implements and small appliances bow
down to you? Does the TV pick the all-sports
channel for you and the fridge keep your beer cold
without your even asking? Go ahead, fart out loud,
flick your boogers on the floor. And if you take
a notion to dance naked in front of the hallway
mirror, that's OK, too.

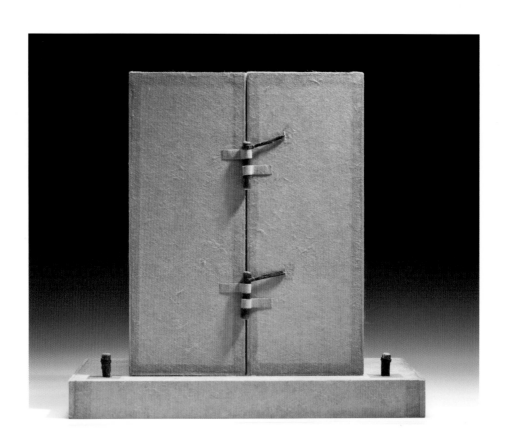

Temple

My first home in the woods was in the backyard under the
forsythia bushes, a warm green cave I could crawl into and not
be found out, content until suppertime. Since then there have
been others tucked off the back roads and walking trails, places
I knew as soon as I entered in to them. All the woods are full
of such places if you only look, places where you can fetch up
under the high trees and find refuge.

Campanile II

Heading westward, we forget what we are leaving
behind us. Passionate expectation is a necessity
we have to work at, work to save ourselves from
falling into regret. The lay of the hills against the
sky, the path down by the creekside, those we
love… we will never see again. Yes, we must tear
away from all we know for a promise.

Spirit

One must think of Yeats; there's no getting
around it. Lapis, gold, a little bird singing
its heart out. In its song is the promise of a
garden, where we check in for a breather and
just stop time or at least bring it back round
in a circle. There is no garden, there is no
stopping, so just sing along with the birdie.
Best to make joyful sounds all the same.

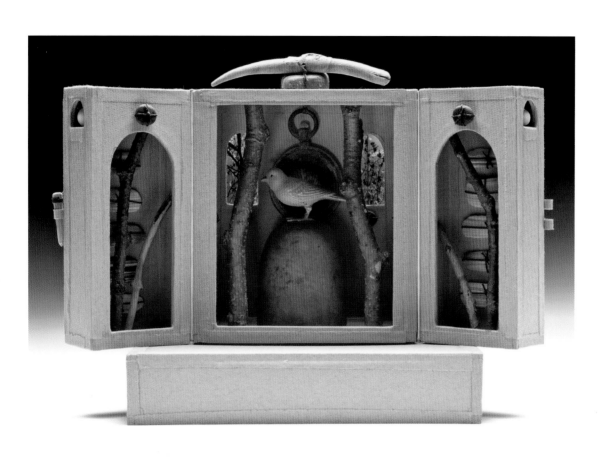

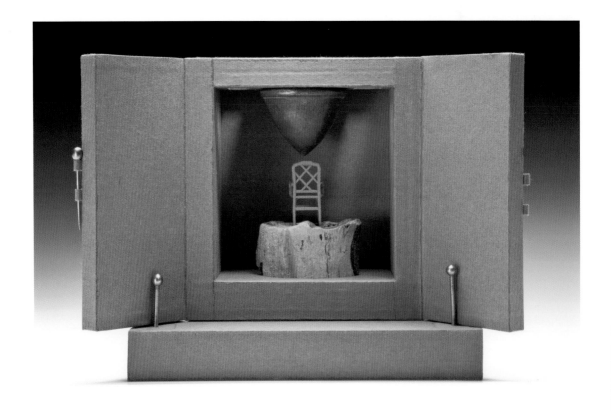

Inbound

This was not punishment, not for me, to be left alone
in communion with the wall, to worry out its shapes,
its textures, its continents and seas. To see past its
blankness to what is really there.

Alaska

Unknown Place

Before I ever broke my leg, I went crooked. In
marching band, the kid behind me, a drummer,
hollered, "Boy, walk straight, dammit," and hit
me with his stick to let me know he meant it.
So it went, each step an accidental landing in
an unexpected place. No, I did not fall so often,
just wound up someplace other than I'd hoped
for—jagged rocks, mud, dog doo. Left only to my
thoughts, though, I would have flown up, away,
clean as an arrow.

Indian River Run

This is how the world got made, made so slowly, so secretly that we hardly noticed. One drop of water on a rock, then another. Pretty soon a river. Then bugs, fish, and the people to catch and eat them.

What happens next will not be slow at all, but sudden. We will only notice when it's gone.

Snow Country

I got lost in the woods once. Not in a metaphysical symbolic way like Dante. In fact, I didn't get lost at all, it was more of a temporary dislocation. I came out in a swampy place where the thin fall ice broke under my footsteps, and I just kept walking, taking it on faith that I'd find my way. The blare of the train's horn, the clank and clatter of the rolling freight straightened me out, talking me home.

Stick Eater

What if your teeth were made to grow and never stop
growing so the only thing you could do was to eat
the world away one stick at a time? What if you were
kind of apologetic about it at first, but later just got
mad as hell? I mean, what kind of life would it be to
consume your life right out from under yourself.

What kind of life would that be?

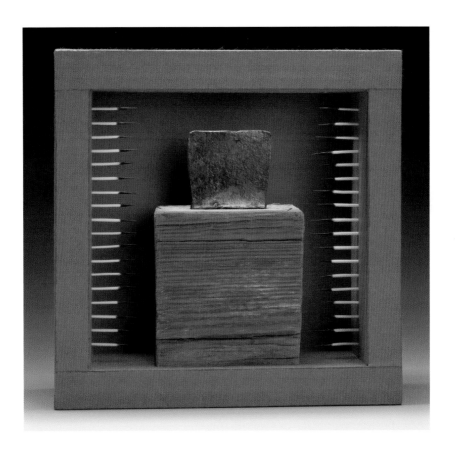

January Light

We come here expecting to find the witch's house, don't we?
These are the woods of a dark winter's day, haunted woods.
There is something down in our limbic brains that says
beware, that says we don't have many friends out in the trees,
that folks who live among them are only those we've cast out.

It just goes to show how wrong we can be. Maybe if we ask
real nice, those in hiding would come out and share their
secrets with us. The woods might enfold us once again.
Maybe we would learn something.

Early Snow

Remember when it snowed early that time? I think it was the
fall of '92. It bent the trees still full of leaves over just like that.
My father was in the hospital, far away, having his chest cut
open, his heart repaired. That day, he almost didn't make it.

Come spring, we all thought the trees would right themselves,
straighten right up. But they didn't. They never did.

Afterword

Boxes, small worlds of wonder made from paper, board, and everyday objects transformed to talismans. And words, just as tautly crafted, just as constrained in scale and expansive in allusion, calling into form companion spheres of memory and experience that intersect with the visual realms they adjoin.

The intersections are various, now illuminating, now confounding. The space between sensibilities is bridged again and again by art, intimacy, and a shared experience that is more about exploration than long familiarity. Encountering the art of Margo Klass and Frank Soos in this volume is a lot like attending an exhibition of their work in a gallery, alone. Their work is rich with reference, suggestion, reticence, and revelation, and it requires patience and pondering.

Here, as in the gallery, I begin by looking. I adjust my sensibility to the intimate scale of an individual construction. I come close, letting the rest of the world drop away as I enter the formal and narrative reality of the piece, and it no longer seems small, because it has become the universe into which I've been invited to peer.

Even as I surrender to that realm, I am mindful of the context in which I necessarily see it. Countless collages studied in the past, assemblages of found objects and imagery. Artists' books—which in their fine craftsmanship, inventive technology, and engineering—provide an equally important, different lens. Asian, especially Japanese, sensibility, which I know is the product not just of predilection but of travel and study on the part of the artist.

These and other lenses enrich my view of what I see, and they provide the comfort of context, but they neither constrain nor explain.

Images and objects find their places, varying dizzily in character and scale. As in a poem, the conjoined images infer, rather than spell out, narrative. It is impossible to resist the desire to construct a story of these disparate elements, but they are finely calibrated to make such construction challenging.

I say "challenging," but these are remarkably quiet works, serenely confident rather than invasive. They don't shout for attention. They don't make demands. Instead, they bestow gifts. They reward contemplation. The more I look—the more patient I am with letting them unfold in relation to my own experience—the more they suggest. So I try to be patient. I try not to glance toward the panoply of surrounding sculptures, to keep from looking ahead. And I especially try to put off reading Frank's words, until I can't stand waiting any longer.

I wait because I know that when I read his words, new doors will open, and though I won't be herded into a single, narrow meaning, I will be led in new directions. I'll see this sculpture through his eyes, the arc of his experience, both with Margo and apart from her. I relish that, but I want to put it off until I've made of it what I can out of my own experience.

62

When I do give in, the land Frank's words open is as rich as the artwork to which he responds. It is territory like and unlike that which Margo revealed. The mysteries they explore are the same—place, meaning, family, spirit, love, loss, memory. But their lives have led them through different country, made them different people, brought them to explore these mysteries together, but from very different perspectives and in very different ways.

As constrained in scale as Margo's visual constructions, Frank's verbal ones are similarly dense, as carefully composed, as finely calibrated for suggestion rather than elucidation. But they are wholly different in manner. No matter how humble, how embellished by the patina of wear their elements, Margo's sculptures are elegant, beautiful, their contents exquisite in their presentation. Niches turn lures to amulets, rocks to stelae, faucet to font. Beside them, Frank's words skewer portent, remind us of flesh, of folly, of the foibles and absurdities that engender and undermine our dreams. His words ground oxidation in rust, silence in recollected noise, faith in doubt and resignation.

Frank's words deepen the mysteries, not undermining them but connecting the life of the spirit to the life of the body. He reminds us that the sensual is often carnal, that there is a fine line between gratification and indulgence, that we have to take our refuge where we find it. He grounds her, and she lifts him up.

When I see their work, I hear them talking. Though side by side and hand in hand, they whisper messages across a firth, and I am grateful to be able to catch some of their conversation on the wind.

Kesler Woodward

List of Works

Mixed media constructions

Apparently Never
2002
13 x 10 x 5 in.
PRIVATE COLLECTION,
FAIRBANKS, ALASKA

Balancing Act
2005
24 x 11 x 5 in.

Breaking Forth
2002
9.5 x 7 x 4.5 in.
PRIVATE COLLECTION,
FAIRBANKS, ALASKA

Campanile II
2007
13.5 x 14 x 9 in.

Celestial Navigation
2005
18 x 8.25 x 5 in.

Commerce 123
1998
12 x 14 x 12 in.

Crowley Island Fog
2006
10.25 x 5.25 x 2.5 in.
PRIVATE COLLECTION,
COREA, MAINE

Double Moon
2004
9 x 15.5 x 4 in.

Early Snow
2006
10 x 13 x 6 in.

First Snow
2007
12.5 x 28 x 7.5 in.

Flying Red Point
2004
6 x 13 x 5 in.
PRIVATE COLLECTION,
FAIRBANKS, ALASKA

Gate Way
2005
13.25 x 14.75 x 7.5 in.

Grace
2002
8 x 6 x 4 in.
PRIVATE COLLECTION,
RICHMOND, VIRGINIA

I Dreamed of Ships
2006
16 x 14 x 4.75 in.
PRIVATE COLLECTION

I Have Two
2002
10 x 6.5 x 5 in.

Icon
2006
18 x 9.5 x 5 in.
PRIVATE COLLECTION,
FAIRBANKS, ALASKA

Inbound
2005
8 x 12 x 5.5 in.

Indian River Run
2007
14.5 x 9 x 4 in.
PRIVATE COLLECTION

Jacob's Ladder
2007
27 x 8 x 6.75 in.

January Light
2007
9 x 14 x 4.5 in.

*Learning to Love in a Language
We Do Not Understand*
2005
11.25 x 12 x 6.25 in.

Pavilion
2003
7 x 26 x 2 in.

Permanent Press
2006
17 x 7.5 x 4 in.

Red Herring
2007
8 x 10.5 x 3 in.
PRIVATE COLLECTION,
COREA, MAINE

*Reliquary of St. Sid:
Patron Saint of Surfeit*
2006
12 x 16 x 8 in.

Resurrection
1995
12 x 14 x 12 in.

Rock Paper Scissors III
2007
8 x 7.75 x 3.5 in.
PRIVATE COLLECTION,
FAIRBANKS, ALASKA

Rube
2007
6.25 x 5 x 2 in.
PRIVATE COLLECTION,
FAIRBANKS, ALASKA

Sanctum Sanctorum
2007
10.5 x 11.5 x 7 in.

Site Line
2007
10.5 x 11 x 4 in.

Snow Country
2005
18.75 x 11.5 x 6.25 in.

Something Like That
2003
12 x 13 x 6 in.

Something Not at All Myself
2002
11 x 7 x 5 in.
PRIVATE COLLECTION,
BETHESDA, MARYLAND

Spirit
1995
12 x 15 x 12 in.
PRIVATE COLLECTION,
FAIRBANKS, ALASKA

Staying Still
2007
9.5 x 9.5 x 4 in.

Stick Eater
2007
9.5 x 9.5 x 4 in.

Sugimoto I
2006
15.5 x 15 x 7.25 in.

Tatami Room II
2007
8.75 x 6.25 x 3.5 in.
PRIVATE COLLECTION,
FAIRBANKS, ALASKA

Teahouse
2004
10.75 x 7.25 x 5.75 in.
COLLECTION, UNIVERSITY OF
ALASKA MUSEUM OF THE NORTH

Temple
2004
10 x 14 x 6.5 in.
PRIVATE COLLECTION,
FAIRBANKS, ALASKA

Three
2007
8.5 x 4.5 x 2.5 in.
PRIVATE COLLECTION,
MOUNT DESERT, MAINE

Unknown Place
2005
11.5 x 9.5 x 6 in.

Warrior
2002
13 x 7 x 4.5 in.

Window Over the Couch
2005
10 x 12 x 4 in.
PRIVATE COLLECTION,
FAIRBANKS, ALASKA

Acknowledgments

We would like to thank our countless friends, colleagues, and family members for their encouragement and support of our work and would like to extend very special thanks to the following: Kes Woodward, Dickson Carroll, and Jack Boul for Margo's artistic support; Kes Woodward, Peggy Shumaker, and Janis Lull for Frank's. Thanks to Deborah Sokolove and the Dadian Gallery in Washington, D.C., for presenting our first collaborative exhibit. Thanks to Kate Gale and Mark Cull at Red Hen Press, and once again to Peggy Shumaker and Boreal Books for providing our work a home between book covers. We are especially grateful to Wanda Chin for her elegant book design. And lastly, but significantly, we would thank our friends at the Virginia Center for the Creative Arts both for giving us studio space, support, and encouragement, and for offering us a place where our involved collaboration started and flourished to what it has become today.

Grace

What do we say when we say grace? The harrow breaks the earth, brittle bits of what once was bone and flesh. Old life cut down and turned under. Fire would claim all but leaves char and ash.

Something remains to take to hand. The rock too stubborn to be broken, the hardened knot. In holding them, we know two hard things at once. One is, we were, it is. Harrowed, charred, reduced to the smallest pieces, who are the ones we love now? Still, we must be hopeful, thinking on what has been left, something hard, solid as the earth, nearing perfection.

What do we say when we say grace? Say, grace.